W9-BKT-763

PRINTED IN U.S.A.

A BROWNING HANDBOOK

ROBERT BROWNING AT THE AGE OF 47

From a drawing made by Field Talfourd at Rome in 1859. Reproduced
by the courtesy of the National Portrait Gallery.

A
BROWNING
HANDBOOK

by

William Clyde DeVane

YALE UNIVERSITY

SECOND  EDITION

NEW YORK

Appleton-Century-Crofts, Inc.

66-4905

674-3

Library of Congress Card Number:

54-9558

❧ PREFACE ❧

WHEN the first edition of this *Browning Handbook* was projected, twenty-five years ago, a smaller and more general book was planned. But a closer view of the scholarship which had been done upon Browning's poetry convinced me that the subject required above all else a complete and detailed treatment. An excellent biography of the poet had been written, a great number of the poet's letters had been collected, and a fair number of special studies, some of excellent quality, had been made of Browning's ideas and of separate poems. But the treatment was uneven; many of the ideas and poems were inadequately dealt with, and others were not accounted for at all. The results, moreover, were scattered in a hundred different places. Browning scholarship, in short, was not mature in the sense that the scholarship upon Chaucer, Spenser, Shakespeare, Milton, or even Wordsworth, was mature. I became convinced that what Browning scholarship needed most of all was the assembling and arrangement of all the pertinent facts concerning each one of the poems; and to accomplish this was the aim of the work. The task was too huge to be done perfectly, but it was done painstakingly. The book would serve, I hoped, as a convenient collection of materials towards the interpretation of Browning and his works, and as a point of departure for further investigations.

Factual and specific as the book aimed to be, however, I was unwilling to ignore the larger aspects of the problem, the development of the mind of Robert Browning. In my treatment of the poems I therefore adopted the chronological order of their publication—which with Browning follows closely the order of writing—in preference to the poet's later and somewhat arbitrary grouping of his poems. Charles Lamb's judgment upon Wordsworth's comparable attempt to build his poems into larger unities still seems to me to have been a good one: "There is only one good order, and that is the order

in which they were written. That is the history of the poet's mind."
The arrangement of the present edition follows the same principle.
Thus while the reader seeking information about a particular poem
will be able to find the facts readily by means of the index, the student
who cares to read the volume consecutively will find, I think, if he
will pardon the repetitions necessary to a handbook arrangement, a
detailed and circumstantial account of the poet's progress in his
thinking, his art, and his reputation.

The hope I expressed in my first edition, that the *Handbook* would
serve as a point of departure for further investigations, has been fully
answered in the intervening years, as the reader may see from the
many additions and corrections which have been made in this new
edition. The great quantity of new material has made the revision a
major task. Browning scholarship has not only increased in bulk and
variety, but has, I believe, proportionately improved in quality. Several new biographies have been published; collections of hitherto un-
published letters have become available, and old letters have been
re-edited; and many excellent special studies of the poet's life and
work have appeared in books and learned journals. These are duly
used and acknowledged, I trust, in the text, footnotes, and bibliography of the present edition of this *Handbook*.

Because my debt still stands and it is pleasant to acknowledge
again, I should like to repeat here the paragraphs of thanks which I
recorded in my Preface to the first edition in 1935:

"My study of Browning's poetry has led me into many pleasant
places, and I cannot forego mentioning here the unfailing kindnesses
which I have encountered abroad in the British Museum, the Bod-
leian, the Balliol College Library, the Victoria and Albert Museum,
and the equal spirit of help which I have found at home, especially in
the library of Yale University where this work was chiefly conducted,
and in the library of Cornell University where it was finished. I have
been graciously permitted to consult the manuscripts and letters in
the Wellesley College Library and in the Pierpont Morgan Library in
New York City, and have had the privilege of access to the private
collections of Professors Chauncey Brewster Tinker and William
Lyon Phelps.

"A full record of my indebtednesses would make this preface grotesque. As much of my debt as I could, I have declared in my list of
acknowledgments below, in my footnotes, and in my bibliography.
But I ought to express here my general reliance upon the admirable

biography of the poet by Messrs. Griffin and Minchin. The student of Browning must be grateful steadily to Sir Frederic Kenyon for his great edition [the *Centenary Edition*] of the poems and for collecting the letters of the poet and his wife; in America, Professor A. J. Armstrong made available in 1923 the illuminating letters which Browning wrote to his friend, Miss Blagden,[1] and in 1933 Dean T. L. Hood earned the gratitude of all students of the poet by making accessible and editing the letters collected by Mr. T. J. Wise, together with a number of his own. To all these I owe much. But there are subtler debts. In spite of my attempts to be independent many of my former students will recognize ideas which are probably and justly their own. The list is long, and will some day be distinguished, and it is not from ingratitude that I do not make a roll-call here. Upon the greatest and subtlest of all my debts, I am forced to bless myself with silence.

"Finally, it is a pleasure to record the generosity of authors and publishers in granting permission to use materials from their works. My thanks are due to Mr. H. C. Minchin for the privilege of quoting from his book, *The Life of Robert Browning;* to the Houghton Mifflin Co. for permission to quote from the revised edition of Mrs. Orr's *Life and Letters of Robert Browning;* to The Macmillan Company for the use of the *Complete Poetical Works of Robert Browning, New Edition, with Additional Poems;* to Dean T. L. Hood and Sir John Murray for permission to quote from *Letters of Robert Browning, Collected by T. J. Wise;* to the Harper and Bros. Co. for *Letters of Robert Browning and Elizabeth Barrett Barrett;* to Professor A. J. Armstrong for the use of *Letters of Robert Browning to Isa Blagden;* to the E. P. Dutton Company for permission to quote from *Elizabeth Barrett Browning; Letters to her Sister,* edited by Leonard Huxley; to the Oxford University Press for Mr. A. K. Cook's *Commentary on Browning's "The Ring and the Book";* to the Yale University Press for permission to use my own book, *Browning's Parleyings;* to Messrs. G. Bell and Sons and Harcourt, Brace and Co. for Mrs. Orr's *Handbook to Browning's Works;* to Messrs. Chapman and Hall for the use of *The Diaries of W. C. Macready,* edited by William Toynbee; to Charles Scribner's Sons for permission to quote from the Blashfield and Hopkins edition

---

[1] These letters have since been edited by Edward C. McAleer in 1951 with the title, *Dearest Isa, Robert Browning's Letters to Isabella Blagden,* and published by the University of Texas Press. With Mr. McAleer's kind permission my references are to his edition throughout.

of Vasari's *Lives of Seventy Most Eminent Painters;* and to the National Portrait Gallery for permission to reproduce the portrait of Browning which serves as frontispiece."

Since the first edition my debt of gratitude has greatly increased. I take great pleasure in expressing my thanks to the John Simon Guggenheim Memorial Foundation and to Yale University for making possible the leisure necessary to complete this work. I must again record my gratitude to the Yale University Library for the use of its rich resources and the help of its efficient staff. The roll-call of my students is longer now, and has grown in distinction, and my debt is constantly increasing. I should like also to thank my colleagues, Professors Richard L. Purdy, Gordon S. Haight, and Alexander M. Witherspoon, for their help with many details.

I should like especially to thank Professor Kenneth L. Knickerbocker whose labors on our *New Letters of Robert Browning* added much to my knowledge. I should also like to record my appreciation of the work of Professor W. O. Raymond, whose steady and luminous judgment has been a beacon to Browning scholars for many years. For that other deeper and subtler debt, greater than all these together, I still have no adequate words.

W. C. DeV.

❧ CONTENTS ❧

A BROWNING HANDBOOK

A word about the mechanics of using this *Handbook*. Many books useful for background are listed in the Bibliography, which are not mentioned in the text or notes. On the other hand, a few frequently used books are referred to in the notes by abbreviated titles, the key to which is given in the Bibliography. In some cases, no footnote is given if the reference in the text makes the reference clear; for example, letters that can easily be located by date are given no page citations; these volumes too can be found by recourse to the Bibliography.

The notes are numbered consecutively throughout the discussion of each of Browning's large titles, except for *Men and Women*, which is divided into Volumes I and II for convenience in numbering the notes. Cross references to notes within the same group are by note number; otherwise to separate poems by name.

❧ I ❧

THE
LIFE OF ROBERT BROWNING

❧❧❧❧❧❧❧❧❧❧❧❧❧❧❧❧❧❧❧❧❧❧❧❧❧❧❧❧

I

WHEN Harry Bailly and his company of pilgrims set out from the Tabard Inn at Southwark at sunrise on the morning of April 17, 1386, Geoffrey Chaucer might have peered towards the south in the uncertain morning light and seen the place where, in the course of long time, on May 7, 1812, Robert Browning was born. Camberwell, across the Thames from the main part of London, is today a confused mass of bricks and chimney-pots; there are mean streets and squalid alleys; the desperate poor drive a petty trade in those slums, and the grinding noise of motor-busses seldom ceases. In a short time after leaving the Tabard, Harry Bailly brought his company to the little brook called St. Thomas-a-Watering; he was in the open country and could see the line of road ahead, the trees and the flowers, and even the soft April sun, if indeed the "shoures sote" were not falling at the moment. The Camberwell upon which Browning opened his eyes in 1812 was not the same scene that Chaucer saw, but it had changed less, perhaps, between 1386 and 1812 than it has since that time. When Browning was a boy it was a suburb of the middle classes, with comfortable detached houses here and there, a village green, and a square church-tower that was visible from the Strand, three miles away. Across the meadows from Camberwell a "green half-hour's walk" was Dulwich with its then famous gallery of paintings, and not far away was Dulwich Wood, the haunt of gypsies. Into this pleasant and convenient world Robert Browning was born.

Because of the darkness of Browning's hair and the pallor of his

1

complexion, in both of which he was matched by his sister Sarianna, two years younger than himself, it was the fashion of the older biographers to imagine that he had Jewish or Creole blood in his veins. The first of these suppositions seems founded on nothing more substantial than the facts that two of Browning's uncles were employed in the Rothschild banking houses in London and Paris, and that in later years the poet delighted in rabbinical lore. The legend of Creole blood is hardly more substantial: his grandmother, Margaret Tittle Browning, had been born and bred in the West Indies of an English family. The Brownings came from the substantial yeomanry of Dorset. The poet's grandfather, Robert Browning,[1] was born in 1749 in Pentridge, a small village in northeastern Dorset. He came to London in the last third of the eighteenth century and was a respectable harbinger of that excellent middle class which by the great industrial and economic revolution of the nineteenth century was to own and rule England for nearly a hundred years. The Browning family history reminds one strangely of Galsworthy's family of Forsytes, though the Forsytes would never have thought that they could afford a poet, and a man of genius seems to have been beyond their powers to produce.

This Robert Browning was handsome, vigorous, and capable. He began as a clerk in the Bank of England and rose to be the head of a department with a salary of approximately £500 a year. He was an irascible and strong-willed man, and in time planted his sons by his first and second marriages, their aptitudes hardly considered, in positions in his own business of banking. His oldest son, Robert Browning (1782–1866), the father of the poet, was sent out at the age of twenty to a lucrative position at St. Kitt's, his mother's sugar plantation in the West Indies. But there, as the poet told Miss Barrett many years later,

[he] conceived such a hatred of the slave system . . . that he relinquished every prospect—supported himself, while there, in some other capacity, and came back, while yet a boy, to his father's profound astonishment and rage—one proof of which was, that when he heard that his son was a suitor to *her*, my mother—he benevolently waited on her uncle to assure him that his niece would be thrown away on a man so evidently born to be hanged!— those were his words. My father on his return had the intention of devoting himself to art, for which he had many qualifications and abundant love —but the quarrel with his father,—who married again and continued to

---

[1] See Sir Vincent Baddeley, "The Ancestry of Robert Browning, the Poet," in the *Genealogists Magazine* 8:1–6 (March, 1938).

hate him till a few years before his death,—induced him to go at once and consume his life after a fashion he always detested.[2]

The young man took a place as clerk in the Bank of England on his return from St. Kitt's and remained there as a superior clerk until his retirement in 1852. He was married to the poet's mother, Sarah Anna Wiedemann, in Camberwell on February 19, 1811, without the sanction of his angry father.

One may well believe that the poet's father merely endured the business of banking. He was at heart an artist, a scholar, and a collector of books and pictures. A considerable number of his drawings for his son, and later for his grandson, remain to us: they are mainly illustrations of stories—grotesque groups gather in a cave around a flickering candle, or sudden fierce expressive faces scowl at us from the fly-leaves of old books. In his collection of pictures his preference ran to the Dutch realists; "Brouwer, Ostade, Teniers—he would turn from the Sistine altar-piece to these," said his son. Naturally, among English artists Hogarth was his special love. The verses which he wrote were of the same kind, anecdotes in jocular verse written for children. His version of the story of the Pied Piper, though inferior, has all the qualities of his son's poem upon the same subject.[3] His taste in serious verse was for the couplets of Pope and the eighteenth century. As a student he had a strong leaning towards curious and out-of-the-way history. He had the scent of the collector for rare books, and the 6000 volumes of his library were made up of many of the substantial and important books of the world.[4] They were in Greek, Hebrew, Latin, French, Italian, and Spanish, and his annotations show that they were read as well as bought. There were also in the library a great number of collections of astonishing anecdotes, culled from all history; the example and archetype of these was Nathaniel Wanley's *Wonders of the Little World*, 1678, from which the poet gleaned much. There were also a considerable number of biographical dictionaries, such as the *Biographie universelle*, 1822, whose fifty volumes seem to have been read *in toto* by the poet.[5] In his hours of leisure from the bank the elder Browning

[2] *Letters of Robert Browning and Elizabeth Barrett Barrett, 1845–6*, II, 477.
[3] It was printed in *The Bookman* (London) for May, 1912.
[4] See the auction catalogue of Sotheby, Wilkinson and Hodge, generally known as *The Browning Collections,* which was published upon the dispersal of the Browning library in 1913.
[5] *The Life of Robert Browning* . . . by W. Hall Griffin, completed and edited by Harry Christopher Minchin, 1938, p. 25.

seems to have read most of these books; his half-brother, Reuben, called him a "living encyclopaedia." He could write out his own notion of the story of Sordello in prose, and in his old age could produce a "regular bookful of notes and extracts" for the use of his son in the historical parts of *The Ring and the Book*.[6] One can see that Browning got many traits from this genial and accomplished man, "who," in the son's words, "might have been a great man had he cared a bit about it." But he did not care enough to assert himself. The good, kindly, unworldly man was content to take his place in the family as a docile child, willing to follow where his wife led, and submitting to the will of his far more aggressive children, Robert and Sarianna.

The poet's mother was more influential in shaping the boy's character. As her name implies, Sarah Anna Wiedemann was of German descent. Her father was a native of Hamburg, connected with shipping; he lived in Dundee and had married a Scotch lady. The poet's father met Miss Wiedemann when she and her sister, Christiana, were living in Camberwell with an uncle. Christiana married John Silverthorne, a wealthy brewer of the neighborhood, and her sons, James, John, and George, became the constant companions of Browning's youth. Mrs. Browning, whom Carlyle called "the true type of a Scottish gentlewoman," seems to have taken charge of the emotional aspects of her son's education. She was an enthusiastic musician, and imparted her delight to her son. She was fond of playing at dusk, and once when she was playing her little son stole downstairs to listen, and when she had ceased flung himself into her arms, sobbing "Play, play." [7] From his mother, too, Browning learned to love flowers and to know the peculiar pleasure of making friends with all the small animals of the garden, as well as the larger ones of the house and stable. He was often bribed to take his medicine by the promise of a toad or a spider which his mother would find for him among her flowers. But above all, Mrs. Browning gave her son her piety. She was a member of the Congregational Church of York Street, Walworth, where her children were christened, and in time she brought to the chapel her husband, who, something of an eighteenth-century rationalist, had not been as devout in his early days as he later became. Her children attended regularly, but not always eagerly. This good, gentle, evangelical Christian inculcated

[6] *Idem*, pp. 17–8, 98–9.
[7] *Idem*, p. 17.

her doctrine in her son, and he became "passionately religious," as
he described himself in his later years. From her teachings he never
entirely broke free, save in the boyish rebellion which Shelley and
Voltaire gave him license for, and the quelling of that revolt is the
theme of *Pauline,* his first published book. Browning adored his
mother, and when she died in 1849 while he was in Italy, he did not
lightly recover from the loss.[8] Such, then, were the parents of the
poet, whom Carlyle described as "people of respectable position
among the dissenters, but not rich neither."

II

In this world the boy grew, playing in the fields and woods by day,
and at night-fall hearing his mother play upon the piano or his father
chant the odes of Anacreon. He began early to paint in currant juice,
and soon after to make verses of his own. He was reading and writing
at five. We get what is probably an authentic piece of biography in
the little poem, *Development,* which Browning published when he
was seventy-seven:

> My father was a scholar and knew Greek.
> When I was five years old, I asked him once
> "What do you read about?"
>   "The siege of Troy."
> "What is a siege and what is Troy?"
>   Whereat
> He piled up chairs and tables for a town,
> Set me a-top for Priam, called our cat
> —Helen, enticed away from home (he said)
> By wicked Paris, who couched somewhere close
> Under the footstool, being cowardly,
> But whom—since she was worth the pains, poor puss—
> Towzer and Tray,—our dogs, the Atreidai,—sought
> By taking Troy to get possession of
> —Always when great Achilles ceased to sulk,
> (My pony in the stable)—forth would prance
> And put to flight Hector—our page-boy's self.

When it was time to send the lad to school he was put in a small
elementary school in the neighborhood. But there he was so far
ahead of the larger boys that he was dismissed to avoid jealousy. He
went back to his father's library and buried himself in such books as

---

[8] For the profound sympathy between Browning and his mother, see Betty
Miller, *Robert Browning, A Portrait,* 1952, pp. 14–6, 157–62, 165.

Quarles' *Emblems* and, later, in Gerard de Lairesse's *The History of Painting in All Its Branches*. It was not long afterwards that he wrote his first formal poem:

the first *composition* I was guilty of was something in *imitation* of Ossian, whom I had not read, but *conceived* through two or three scraps in other books— I never can recollect *not* writing rhymes, but I knew they were nonsense even then; *this*, however, I thought exceedingly well of, and laid up for posterity under the cushion of a great arm-chair. . . . I could not have been five years old, that's one consolation.[9]

When he was eight or nine the boy was sent to school at Peckham to the establishment of the Misses Ready, and later to the Reverend Mr. Thomas Ready. He was boarded by the week at the school, only a mile from his home, and at the end of the week would return with delight to Camberwell. The school made little impression upon him. His chief recollection in later days seems to have been that the Misses Ready oiled and brushed the children's hair once a week to the tunes of Isaac Watts' hymns. Browning was "unluckily precocious," and the school was too easy for him. John Domett, elder brother to Alfred, Browning's friend in later years, remembered

young Browning in a pinafore of brown Holland, such as small boys used to wear in those days, for he was always neat in his dress; and how they used to pit him against much older and bigger boys in a chaffing match to amuse themselves with the little bright-eyed fellow's readiness and acuteness of repartee.[10]

He remained in the school until he was fourteen, and came forth aggressive, self-confident, and not a little self-centered. Perhaps this unlovely aspect of his boyish nature was in his mind when he described that period of his life in *Pauline*, the biographical poem of his twentieth year:

> . . . long restraint chained down
> My soul, till it was changed. I lost myself,
> And were it not that I so loathe that time,
> I could recall how first I learned to turn
> My mind against itself; and the effects,
> In deeds for which remorse were vain, as for
> The wanderings of delirious dream; yet thence
> Came cunning, envy, falsehood.

But this is to anticipate. In the meantime the young scholar had passed, in his twelfth year, beyond Pope's translation of Homer to the

[9] *Letters of Robert Browning and Elizabeth Barrett Barrett*, II, 469.
[10] Quoted in Griffin and Minchin, *Life*, p. 30.

original and, more important for him at the time, he had made the discovery of Byron at almost precisely the ideal age for appreciating that poet's heroic poems. With a modesty which at that time he did not sincerely possess, he gave to a volume of poems which he produced the title of *Incondita*. His parents were delighted, and sent the manuscript about in search of a publisher. Their search was fruitless, needless to say, but not everywhere did the poems fall on stony ground. In the somewhat narrow limits of the society of Liberal Dissenters in which the Brownings moved there were two sisters, the Misses Eliza and Sarah Flower, daughters of Benjamin Flower who for seven years was editor of the *Cambridge Intelligencer*. This paper was devoted to political and religious liberty, and Flower at one time had suffered imprisonment for his opinions. His daughters grew into beautiful young ladies, intellectual, musical, and devout to a degree. Eliza Flower was twenty-two, nine years older than Browning, when *Incondita* came into her hands from her friends at Camberwell, and she and her sister thought well enough of the poems to copy them out, and Sarah Flower chose two poems to send to her guardian, W. J. Fox. These two poems, *The First-Born of Egypt* and *The Dance of Death*, are the only specimens of the volume which escaped Browning's destructive hand.[11] Fox, brought up on the "sour milk of Calvinism" as he described it, was rapidly moving towards Unitarianism. He was a popular preacher of the day, and on the side an editor and a politician of strong Liberal and reforming tendencies. When Browning's poems came into his hands he praised them, but added, a little ponderously, that they showed "too great splendour of language and too little wealth of thought." It was Fox who first reviewed *Pauline* and found a publisher for *Paracelsus*, and became in Browning's words his "literary father." *Incondita* was destroyed by its author, and the only wrack left behind seems to have been that the lad of fourteen lost his heart to Eliza, and wrote verses and letters to her. It was she, as we know from Mrs. Sutherland Orr, who inspired *Pauline* six years later.[12]

[11] The poems, and the letter in which they were enclosed—dated May 31 (1827?)—were first published by Mr. Bertram Dobell in an article in the *Cornhill Magazine* for January, 1914, called "The Earliest Poems of Robert Browning." They are accessible in the *Macmillan Edition*. For Browning's great anxiety to destroy all copies of his early poems see *Letters of Robert Browning, Collected by Thomas J. Wise*, edited by Thurman L. Hood, 1933, pp. 19–20.

[12] *Life and Letters of Robert Browning* by Mrs. Sutherland Orr, New Edition, Revised and in part rewritten by Frederic G. Kenyon, 1908, p. 35. For a fuller account of Eliza Flower see Miller, *Robert Browning*, pp. 29–34, 36–8, 41–4, 47.

It was probably of the *Incondita* that Browning spoke in the lines of *Pauline,* looking back to an earlier time:

> No fear was mine
> As I gazed on the works of mighty bards,
> In the first joy at finding my own thoughts
> Recorded, and my powers exemplified,
> And feeling their aspirings were my own.

The *Incondita* was indubitably a series of imitations, probably chiefly of Byron, but the poems were surely not so utterly devoid of promise as their adolescent or their aged author imagined. In technical skill and native talent the young poet's lines upon *The First-Born of Egypt* are not unworthy to stand by the youthful Tennyson's lines in *The Devil and the Lady.*

Browning's formal education was practically at an end when he left Mr. Ready's school at the age of fourteen. Henceforth his school-room was his father's library. The boy was probably instructed by his father in Latin and Greek; he had a private tutor in French, and Angelo Cerutti was his teacher in Italian. In music he came in time under the tutelage of "great John Relfe," musician-in-ordinary to the king. His singing master was Isaac Nathan, author of the *Hebrew Melodies,* who entertained him with anecdotes of Byron. For the rest, he was "free as a stag" in the woods and fields, and the range of his father's bookshelves was his own. Across the fields was the Dulwich Gallery, and three miles away were the theaters and the excitements of London. Meanwhile he could lie on the grassy tops of Camberwell's little hills and see a good deal of the world. When the new University of London was opened in 1828 young Browning was enrolled to take Greek, Latin, and German, and quarters were engaged for him in Bedford Square. One week of Bloomsbury was enough, and after a little more than half a year the university lost one of its most distinguished pupils, and the elder Browning had lost £100. In their circumstances the Brownings probably expected their son to prepare himself for a profession, and they favored the law for him. He announced his intention to be a poet. Many good battles, as he later said, had to be fought, but his will was stronger than his family's. He was dependent upon his father for all the necessities of life until his marriage in 1846. Well might the poet tell Miss Barrett that he had been " 'spoiled' in this world" by his fond and indulgent parents.

Meanwhile his development into a cocksure and self-centered

youngster had caused his parents and friends no little pain. As a boy he had been publicly rebuked in church for his behavior. When he was fourteen he came upon the works of Voltaire and Shelley, and he rapidly became a vegetarian, a scoffer, an atheist and, as Mrs. Orr tells us, "gratuitously proclaimed himself everything that he was, and some things that he was not." [13] Not finding enough game at home, he sought out Sarah Flower, with what effect we may see from a touching letter which that lady wrote to her guardian, the Reverend Mr. Fox, in November of 1827:

> My mind has been wandering a long time, and now it seems to have lost sight of that only invulnerable hold against the assaults of this warring world, a firm belief in the genuineness of the Scriptures. . . . The cloud has come over me gradually, and I did not discover the darkness in which my soul was shrouded until, in seeking to give light to others, my own gloomy state became too settled to admit of doubt. It was in answering Robert Browning that my mind refused to bring forward argument, turned recreant, and sided with the enemy. . . . [14]

Sarah Flower lived to recover her faith and to write *Nearer, My God, to Thee;* the Griffin and Minchin biography wittily remarks that "Robert Browning may reasonably be said to have contributed to the evolution of this famous hymn."

The true story of Browning's discovery of Shelley's poetry has, after many misguided statements, been told.[15] There is no doubt that in time Browning read "Mr. Shelley's atheistical works," but there is equally no doubt that his first acquaintance with Shelley was through the little pirated edition of the lyrics, published by Benbow in 1826. The volume, called *Miscellaneous Poems,* was given to him by his cousin James Silverthorne soon after its publication, and it is a touch of irony that the poet's mother bought for him the inflammatory *Queen Mab.* Shelley's influence was to last for many years, and was, in all, to be the most potent literary influence which Browning ever experienced. In *Pauline* he represents himself as having escaped from the subversive religious thought of Shelley; but surely not before 1855 was he free from the poetic thought of the Sun-treader, if indeed he ever entirely escaped. The glorious discovery is chronicled in *Pauline,* and it is significant that Browning there at once repudiates and yet follows adoringly his master. It is

[13] Orr, *Life,* p. 43.
[14] Moncure D. Conway, *Centenary of South Place,* 1894, p. 46.
[15] See F. A. Pottle's ingenious study, *Shelley and Browning, A Myth and Some Facts,* Chicago, 1923.

enough to say here that Shelley made Browning the poet he was; he gave him poetical and political ideas, method and technique, and pointed out that the proper subject of poetry is the soul of the poet himself. Thus Browning arrived at his first definition of his art:

> And then thou said'st a perfect bard was one
> Who shadowed out the stages of all life. . . .[16]

In this mood the young man had quit the university, and now began vigorously to prosecute his "plan to look on real life."

Real life included a good deal: riding, dancing, singing, fencing, and boxing were essential parts of it, and attendance upon Dr. Blundell's medical lectures at Guy's Hospital seems not to have been excluded. The best of all places to see real life was in the theater, and many "warm moon-births and long evening ends" saw him walking from London with his cousin James Silverthorne. Coming home from Kean's performance of *Richard III* at Richmond on October 22, 1832, exalted with youth and ambition, he conceived the grandiose plan of writing a poem, an opera, a novel, under fictitious names, and the world was never to guess that all these were from one hand. *Pauline* was to be the work of the poet. In January, 1833, the poem was done, and his aunt, Mrs. Silverthorne, provided the £30 necessary for its publication. It appeared anonymously in March, under the imprint of Saunders and Otley, and the author sent twelve copies to Fox to be distributed for review. He then waited for the world to acknowledge him. Fox welcomed the young poet with a shout, and Allan Cunningham was enthusiastic in the *Athenaeum;* but not a copy of *Pauline* was sold. After a while the bale of unbound sheets was stored in the Browning attic, and it was many years before the world was to know the author of the little poetical biography.

Pauline, however, did not go entirely unmarked, save by Cunningham and Fox. It is not too bold to say that a review of the poem which was not published at the time altered the direction of Browning's poetical aspirations. Fox had given one of his copies for review to John Stuart Mill, a young man then, whose clear and searching mind was to leave its impress upon the age. Mill prepared the notes for his critique, but when the magazine for which he intended it anticipated him with a brief contemptuous notice of *Pauline,* he returned the volume to Fox with marginal comments and a critical

---

[16] I quote from the first edition. Browning's later change of "shadowed out" to "chronicled" gives an entirely different task to the bard.

summary in the end pages.[17] The keen analytical mind of Mill penetrated immediately the thin disguise of the Latin preface and the French note and saw *Pauline* for what it was, the sincere confession of a young writer who seemed "possessed with a more intense and morbid self-consciousness than I ever knew in any sane man." Mill realized also that "Pauline" was not a real woman, or at any rate that the poet was not in love with her, and the best thing he can wish for the author is that he shall find a real "Pauline." Neither was Mill beguiled by the young poet's pretensions to repentance and reform:

The self-seeking and self-worshipping state is well described—beyond that, I should think the writer had made, as yet, only the next step, viz. into despising his own state. I even question whether part even of that self-disdain is not *assumed*. He is evidently *dissatisfied*, and feels part of the badness of his state; he does not write as if it were purged out of him. If he once could muster a hearty hatred of his selfishness it would *go;* as it is, he feels only the *lack* of *good*, not the positive evil. He feels not remorse, but only disappointment. . . . Meanwhile he should not attempt to show how a person may be *recovered* from this morbid state,—for *he* is hardly convalescent, and "what should we speak of but that which we know?"

This was indeed seeing the young Browning plain.

Fox gave the volume back to Browning, who read Mill's criticism on October 30, 1833, as we know from his entry in the same volume. As he read he realized that he had exposed his callow soul to the gaze of a stranger, a thing hateful to him the rest of his days. The thought of *Pauline* became repugnant to him; he hid it from sight. Henceforward, his poetry would be objective and dramatic, the utterances of created characters, not of himself. The perfect bard hereafter was one who "chronicled" the souls of others, preferably historical persons. At the end of his own note in Mill's copy of *Pauline,* Browning wrote, "Only this crab remains of the shapely Tree of Life in this Fool's paradise of mine."

The whole episode of *Pauline* rankled in the heart of the young poet. The poem itself is, perhaps, an admission of defeat, for Shelley had meant to the young Browning rebellion against his parents, the church, and society. *Pauline* is a record of his capitulation, and in some ways his loss of freedom. As his sister, Sarianna, was to say of this period in Browning's life, "The fact was, poor boy, he had out-

[17] This interesting copy of *Pauline* is in the Forster and Dyce Collection in the Victoria and Albert Museum, where I have seen it. See the admirable account of this part of Browning's career in Griffin and Minchin, *Life,* pp. 55–60. See also Miller, *Robert Browning,* pp. 40–2.

grown his social surroundings. They were absolutely good, but they were narrow; it could not be otherwise, he chafed under them." But his first attempt to break into the large world was not only an utter failure; it had left his rebellion tamed and his pride humbled.

III

Happily, the secret of *Pauline* was known to very few, and the world was yet to see the dramatic poet. He could console himself with the fact that he was only twenty-one, and Mill and the other reviewers had seen beauty and promise in *Pauline*. Meanwhile, in the midst of a devoted family he got on with his convalescence. In the spring of 1834 the opportunity came, possibly through the association of his uncle, Reuben Browning, with the Rothschild banking interests, for the poet to accompany the Chevalier George de Benkhausen, the Russian consul general, to St. Petersburg. On March 1, with his mother's gift, a Bible, in his luggage, Browning set out. The packet took his company to the Low Countries, and from there the journey was made by carriage. In later years he chiefly remembered the versts and versts of pine in the flat country of western Russia. *Ivàn Ivànovitch,* written forty-five years later, shows the impression the country made upon him. He recalled, too, years afterward, the Russian songs he had heard and the flowers he had seen. His whole journey took only two months, and he was at home again by the first of May.

For a while Browning was eager to become a diplomat, and his desires were probably whetted by his new friendship with the Comte Amédée de Ripert-Monclar, an agent for the French royalists in London. It was this gentleman who suggested the subject of Paracelsus to the poet, and in the fall of 1834 Browning began his second published poem. He had already begun *Sordello,* that poem of many vicissitudes which was to haunt him for seven years. Late in the spring of 1835, Fox found a publisher for *Paracelsus,* and in August the book was published at the expense of Robert Browning, senior. The new poem was dramatic in form, and was ornamented with elaborate notes. This time the name of the author appeared on the title-page. The soul exposed purported to be that of the German chemist and physician of the Renaissance, but one can see that the desire to "know," which is the chief characteristic of the hero of the poem, was a quality fully developed in Browning himself, and the crying need to couple "love" with "knowledge" was the trait of an historical personage who was not born until May 7, 1812. Some of the reviewers were not far wrong in seeing Shelley behind the scenes, but the young poet was so sure of his historical accuracy that he challenged his readers in a note. "The liberties I have taken with my subject are very trifling; and the reader may slip the foregoing scenes between the leaves of any memoir of Paracelsus he pleases, by way of commentary." This was to do his invention a grave wrong; but the disguise sufficed, and *Paracelsus* and its author were welcomed into the literary world of London. The sales of the poem were not great, and the reviewers, though John Forster in the *Examiner* and Fox in the *Monthly Repository* hailed the new poet, were not extravagant in their praise. *Paracelsus*, however, made its way among the best literary minds of the day. In November Browning met Macready, the great tragic actor, who wrote in his diary that the young man looked and spoke "more like a youthful poet than any man I ever saw." This friendship was to shape the course of Browning's life during the next ten years, and give a permanent cast to his nature. On the last day of the year Browning was at Elstree, Macready's home, and there met John Forster, the dramatic critic, whose first words to him were, "Did you see a little notice of you I wrote in the *Examiner?*" The little notice was three columns in length. The crowning event of Browning's early literary fame came at a supper given by Sergeant Talfourd in honor of the success of his play, *Ion,* on May 26, 1836. Many literary folk were present, not the least of whom was Walter Savage Landor. The host proposed a toast to the "Poets of England," and among others nominated the author of *Paracelsus*. As the health was drunk, William Wordsworth leaned across the table and said, "I am proud to drink to your health, Mr. Browning!"

To make his cup run over on that memorable evening, as the party was breaking up Macready spoke to the young poet and said, "Will you not write me a tragedy, and save me from going to America?" From this casual request the poet, urged on by his dramatic ambitions and by his friend Forster, embarked upon that effort, which dominated him for the next ten years, to write a play that would be successful on the boards. In one sense it is possible to regret the time which Browning expended in writing plays. That form of literature was not suitable to his genius, and the best he could achieve was excellent closet drama in the manner, but without the life, of the Elizabethans. The time was not altogether propitious, and the poet lavished an intellectual subtlety and an amazingly expressive style upon some of the most melodramatic of plots. But deeper than time and circumstance was the internal fact in Browning's personality, that he could never escape from his habit of introspection, and he was never able to project the feelings, motives, thoughts, and words of his characters onto the public stage in the way in which the theater and its audience naturally demanded. But to call the dramas wasted effort is to miss their real import. Through those unhappy plays we see Browning's peculiar genius clearing magnificently; the poet was working his way through modifications of the drama, such as *Pippa Passes,* towards his true province, the short dramatic poem of the *Dramatic Lyrics, Dramatic Romances,* and *Men and Women.*

Since I give the history of the plays in some detail in the body of my book, I propose here merely to cull the biographical effects of his association with the theater. Browning was lured into the writing of his first play, *Strafford,* by his familiarity with the subject. When Forster was sick and could not complete his prose *Life of Strafford,* which he had begun and got well along by February, 1836, the poet completed it for him. Browning's play, drawn mainly from this material, was acted five times in May, 1837, and enjoyed an indifferent success. His position in the esteem of Macready and Forster was somewhat impaired in the course of preparation and in the performance. On several occasions Browning, working upon *Sordello* as well as upon *Strafford,* appeared to Macready to be "jaded and thought-sick." He was knowing that agony of effort which makes poets martyrs for the sake of men. His curious and lonely education had little prepared him to communicate with the world, or indeed to know what the world thought ordinary or strange. At the conclusion of the *Strafford* incident he thought he would never write another play. The experience, however, was valuable to him in more ways than one, for in his effort to master the history of the "grand epoch," as he called that period between 1621 and 1648 when Parliament was wringing its victories from the Stuarts, he came upon a political philosophy which was to last him for many years. In *Pauline,* under the influence of Shelley, he had vowed himself to the cause of liberty. The struggles of Hampden, Pym, Eliot, and the other Parliamentarians against the tyranny of the Royalists suddenly gave body and meaning to his phrase. This feeling was confirmed by his visit to Venice in 1838; and as a result the Italian peasant girl in

Sordello takes the place of the aristocratic Palma as the true heroine. Henceforth he was a Liberal, a champion of the cause of the people in England, France, or Italy, and could deplore what he regarded as the defection of Wordsworth when in 1843 the bard became poet laureate. But the whirligig of time was to bring in his revenges.

The success enjoyed by *Paracelsus* had done little to chasten the pride of the young man. Mrs. Bridell-Fox, the daughter of W. J. Fox, in writing her recollections of Browning in the *Argosy* for February, 1890, opens a window upon the mood of Browning about the years 1836–7:

I remember . . . when Mr. Browning entered the drawing-room, with a quick light step; and on hearing from me that my father was out, and in fact that nobody was at home but myself, he said: "It's my birthday to-day; I'll wait till they come in," and sitting down to the piano, he added: "If it won't disturb you, I'll play till they do." And as he turned to the instrument, the bells of some neighbouring church suddenly burst out with a frantic merry peal. It seemed, to my childish fancy, as if in response to the remark that it was his birthday. He was then slim and dark, and very handsome; and—may I hint it—just a trifle of a dandy, addicted to lemon-coloured kid-gloves and such things: quite "the glass of fashion and the mould of form." But full of ambition, eager for success, eager for fame, and, what's more, determined to conquer fame and to achieve success.

The hard work and the ill-success of *Strafford* took something of the jauntiness of the young man away, and the fierce struggles to finish *Sordello* and the blank stare of the world upon its appearance in 1840 humbled him even more.

It is possible to see now why *Sordello* was such a chaotic poem. It was written over a period of seven years, and at least four different conceptions are mingled in the final version. Part of the difficulty was that the young poet was attempting to say some things that had never been said in poetry before. But Browning obviously did not know, or in his pride did not care, what the orthodox knowledge of men consisted in, or what co-operation he might expect from readers. He did not realize that *Paracelsus* had been received precisely because of its freedom from real history, and now he packed his new poem with the most remote and tangled history on record. The result is well known. *Sordello* became the jest of English literature, and remained the most incomprehensible poem in the language until some of our own contemporaries got to work. But whoso looks into *Sordello* may find the ruins of once magnificent cities in the lush tropical forests, "by the caper overrooted." The late Sir Edmund Gosse was unusually right in saying of the poem, "It possesses passages of melody and insight, fresh enough, surprising enough to form the whole stock-in-trade of a respectable poet. . . ." [18] *Sordello* was a bold venture in obscurity and subtlety which had the misfortune to be a hundred years ahead of its time.

With the gift of hindsight we can see the necessity which Browning felt to write *Sordello*. Indeed, in his first three long poems, *Pauline, Paracelsus,* and *Sordello,* we see the young man trying to put himself right with God and his world, but most of all seeking to find himself. In *Sordello* especially we see him progressing towards tolerance as he exorcises at last the romantic, impatient utopian that he was, hypnotized by vast visions. [19] He had also to face the problems of communication, methods and means, form and language. In dealing with abstractions he was a "semantic stutterer," [20] and we see him through *Sordello* working, partially and temporarily perhaps, his cure.

The advantages of writing Sordello's story were by-products of the effort. The poem, like a storm, cleared the poet's spirit and led him to *Pippa Passes* and the shorter poems. In search of local color for *Sordello* he took his first journey to Italy in 1838 and saw Venice and Asolo. The country freed his spirit and taught him, somehow, the beauty of simplicity. But in 1840 the disadvantages of having written *Sordello* far outweighed the advantages. The publication of the poem damaged a promising reputation. Browning was in some respects the laughing-stock of the literary clique in London, though men did not laugh in his face. He seems to have lost his hold upon his friends in the sophisticated world, such as Macready and Forster. There were no more healths to the young poet, and instead he was plunged into that semi-obscurity which was to last for nearly twenty-four years. [21] He still had many friends in London, but he was more often to be seen in his mother's garden at Hatcham, and he cultivated more than before his Camberwell friends, "The Colloquials," made up of Alfred Domett, Joseph Arnould, Christopher Dowson, and

[18] *Robert Browning, Personalia,* p. 48.

[19] See Lionel Stevenson, "Tennyson, Browning, and a Romantic Fallacy," in *University of Toronto Quarterly* 13:175–95 (1943–4).

[20] See Stewart W. Holmes, "Browning: Semantic Stutterer," in *PMLA* 60:231–55 (1945).

[21] M. B. Cramer, however, protests this view of Browning's situation in his article, "Browning's Friendships and Fame before Marriage (1833–1846)," in *PMLA* 55:207–30 (1940). There is some justification for his position, but I think he confuses literary with social success.

others less well known. I do not mean to derogate these men. They were as staunch and good in their way as the London set, perhaps better, but they were not in the public eye and their plumage was not so gay. With Domett especially Browning struck up a warm friendship [22] which was to bear delightful fruit in *Waring, Time's Revenges,* and *The Guardian Angel.* When Domett went out of England to New Zealand in May, 1842, on the tide of emigration so indicative of hard times and a smug world, he elicited from Browning some of the best of his letters. On November 8, 1843, Browning wrote Domett, imagining that the far traveller would soon be at home again, "There you walk past our pond-rail (picking up one of the fallen horse-chestnuts), and now our gate-latch clicks, and now— . . . 'Tis worth while running away to be so wished for again."

The early Forties were hard times in England for young men, as one may see from Carlyle's *Past and Present* or Tennyson's *Locksley Hall,* to go no further. In New Zealand one might in time become prime minister, as Domett did, or at least might be free from the cramping social order that had not yet been temporarily rejuvenated by the industrial revolution, on some island of hope in purple seas. Browning decided to stay at home, but his dreams were not so grandiose as they had been ten years earlier. Now he was content, though "vain and ambitious some nights," to pursue the humble way of the poet and publish his plays and poems in the little paper-covered pamphlets, printed in double columns and published by Moxon at a cost to the poet's father of approximately £16 apiece. These are the pamphlets which make up the since famous *Bells and Pomegranates* series which appeared in eight numbers between 1841 and 1846. It began with *Pippa Passes,* that happy blend of his memory of Asolo as he saw it in 1838, his solitary musings in Dulwich Wood, and his experimentation in a freer dramatic technique than the stage at that time allowed. With *Pippa* Browning began to emerge from the shadow of *Sordello,* and he came out into the sunlight, as we can now see, in the shorter poems of the *Dramatic Lyrics* of 1842 and the *Dramatic Romances* of 1845.

In the meantime, the series continued with another desperate attempt at a successful stage play, and in February, 1843, under the most adverse circumstances, *A Blot in the 'Scutcheon* was produced

[22] The whole history of this friendship is recorded in F. G. Kenyon's book, *Robert Browning and Alfred Domett,* London, 1906.

at Macready's theater in Drury Lane without Macready in the cast. The results were the same as those of *Strafford,* save that this time they were magnified. Browning's melodrama, straining too hard to touch the soft hearts of his time in the manner of Bulwer-Lytton, was acted three times to dwindling audiences. In the course of the performances Browning and Macready quarrelled and ceased to speak to each other, and the friendship with Forster was further impaired. Save for one later fling in *Colombe's Birthday* Browning ceased to write for the stage. These were melancholy and somewhat lonely years. Few readers bought his books, and Browning, past his first youth, seemed baffled at every turn. Perhaps he listened for hope to the story of the long struggle towards fame of his new friend of these years, Thomas Carlyle. But Carlyle's encouragement, if hearty at times and tonic, was fitful, and his usual advice to poets was that they should write prose. In the meanwhile, Browning had tried his hand at prose and had written for the *Foreign Quarterly Review* in 1842 a review of a book on Tasso which turned into a passionate defence of Chatterton's good name.[23] His quieter and greater achievement in these years, however, was the slow perfection of the dramatic monologue as a technique for penetrating even to the secret recesses of the heart.

The Brownings moved from Camberwell in December of 1840 to escape from the rapidly filling suburb. They went further out the "interminable Kent road" to New Cross, Hatcham, in Surrey, and it was here that Carlyle came on horseback. He observed from the order in which Browning's room was kept that he was the apple of his mother's eye. There the poet might be seen of a morning in his blue working shirt, with "Polidoro [Caravaggio]'s perfect Andromeda" before him on his desk, the skull and the pet spider who lived therein. Or if the weather were fine, Browning would lie on the grass in his mother's garden while the wind in the horse-chestnut made the flower-castles nod. One may catch the spirit of the place as well as his own mood in the two delightful *Garden Fancies.* In 1844 he was a man of thirty-two, and though he had done some things that the world would remember, he had not fulfilled his promise to himself. The world was a little stale, possibly flat, and undeniably unprofitable. In this mood he remembered Italy. His earlier journeys had been notable for their celerity, but in his second journey to

[23] See Donald Smalley, *Browning's Essay on Chatterton,* edited with Introductory Chapters and Notes, 1948; also my comments below, in Ch. 8.

Italy he was to have more leisure. He was in Naples in September, 1844, whence he had come by ship. He wandered over the Piano di Sorrento and climbed Vico Alvano, and looked down into the clear Mediterranean from a spot near where Shelley had written his *Stanzas in Dejection.* From Naples he went to Rome and saw the monuments of Shelley and Keats, and one day entered the church of S. Prassede. He came home through northern Italy and down the Rhine with his spirit renewed and the subjects of a good many new poems in mind.

During these years he had added new friends. He met "Barry Cornwall," in life Bryan Waller Procter, and was soon welcomed at the brilliant literary salon of Mrs. Procter, "our lady of bitterness." Then too he became the friend of Thomas Hood, and he called upon Leigh Hunt and heard from him of Shelley, Keats, and Byron. He knew Richard Hengist Horne, who had written *Orion,* the "farthing epic," and he was well acquainted with John Kenyon, kinsman to Elizabeth Barrett and an old school-friend of his father.

While Browning was in Italy in the fall of 1844 Miss Barrett had published her *Poems,* and when he read them upon his return he was pleased to find his name linked with those of Wordsworth and the newly great Tennyson in *Lady Geraldine's Courtship:*

Or from Browning some pomegranate which, if cut deep down the middle,
Shows a heart within blood-tinctured of a veined humanity.

Much gratified, and persuaded by Kenyon, he wrote to Miss Barrett on January 10, 1845: "I love your verses with all my heart, dear Miss Barrett," he began, and a little further in the letter he said, "I do, as I say, love these books with all my heart—and I love you too . . . ," surely an auspicious beginning. And thus was begun the celebrated romance which one must read in its fullness in the letters of these poets. It may be said that here at last, as John Stuart Mill had wished years ago, Browning attained complete convalescence.

The letters between Robert Browning and Elizabeth Barrett which tell of the courtship of a year and three-quarters are the richest biographical documents in Browning literature, but assuredly they are not the clearest. "Their letters may be published a hundred times over," says Chesterton, "they will still remain private." This is partly because they are genuine letters, written for a single person, and it takes a keen and patient reader to catch the interplay of their noble and subtle spirits. Love here has to do with the head as much as with the heart, and is all the surer for that. When the correspondence began Elizabeth Barrett was thirty-nine, six years older than Browning, and for some years had been shut in her room at 50 Wimpole Street as a hopeless invalid. "I had done with living, I thought, when you came and sought me out," she was later to write. Her illness was real enough; it was possibly caused by a broken blood-vessel in her lungs. But it was the tyranny of her father that kept her an invalid. The peculiar psychology which made Edward Barrett what he was had as its main constituent the religious, patriarchal conception of the family carried to the point of mania—a conception not unique among latter-day Puritans. He had Scripture for it that the Lord was a jealous God, and Barrett was made in His image. The family was not to be broken by marriage, and therefore the children, who at last had to be named Septimus and Octavius from the sheer scarcity of names, never dared mention the subject though they were approaching forty. Later Elizabeth was to write her new friend concerning marriage:

'If a prince of Eldorado should come, with a pedigree of lineal descent from some signory in the moon in one hand, and a ticket of good-behaviour from the nearest Independent chapel, in the other'—?

'Why even *then*,' said my sister Arabel, 'it would not *do*.' And she was right, and we all agreed that she was right.

But even from this tyranny and from her darkened room, with ivy at the window and her books and the busts of Homer and Chaucer inside, she had made herself an important literary figure of the age. She saw few people, but she wrote innumerable letters, and became as she called herself a "regular Richardson heroine." Not foreseeing that she could not keep Robert Browning a whole postman's beat from her door, she began her correspondence with this "king of the mystics."

The love between them, being true, took the proverbial course. One can see Browning in its earlier stages, before he has seen the lady, ready to fall in love with a voice, and yet obviously struggling against the new thing which will upset a well-planned life. He broke through the first barrier which she raised when on May 20, 1845, he was permitted to see her. On that day between three and four-thirty she lay on her couch and talked with him as he sat in her arm-chair opposite. The match was applied to the train. He wrote a decorous little note that evening hoping that he had not tired her, that he had not talked too loud. She reassured him, and then, to her unmitigated astonishment, she received from him a passionate love-letter. She sent it back to him and begged him to destroy it, which he did. She pointed out to him the difficulties of her position, and begged him to come as a friend, but never to refer to the subject of love again. He submitted because it was his only course. But if assault fails to take the fort, there is always the way of siege if one has world enough and time. Browning had, and his love enveloped her in a hundred ways. Flowers from his mother's garden were constantly on her tables. He brought her news from the great world of London which she could not visit. He gave her a vision of what a full life might be. His conduct, however, had not the masterful assurance about it that is popularly ascribed to it. He knew the anguish and the humilities of love, and was frequently indecisive and dependent. Miss Barrett, indeed, often appears as the stronger person. In the crisis, however, it was his will that prevailed, as barrier after barrier was surmounted; but perhaps he never would have won the citadel if her father had not played into his hands. The doctor had ordered her to Italy for her health; Barrett, though it was declared that she could not hope for a cure without a change, would not consent to her going. Browning was enjoined to silence, but his anger and love burst from him, and this time he won the citadel and all but ran up his flag. Elizabeth Barrett now began to write the *Sonnets from the Portuguese,* though he did not know it, and her burden there, as in her letters, was that she loved him too well to fetter his life with hers.

The rest is history. The course of love was deepened by the infinitely tender, and infinitely old-fashioned, exchange of locks of hair: "The soul's Rialto hath its merchandise." The sylphs fluttered but the lock was cut. Miss Barrett's health improved wonderfully in the mild winter. Browning wanted to lay the case before her father, but that, she knew, would be madness. Slowly they came to the conclusion that in September they would be married and go to Italy.

On September 9, 1846, Barrett issued an edict that the family would remove to the country for a month while the house in Wimpole Street was being repaired. On the 11th Browning paid his last visit to the house. All arrangements were made, and on Saturday, the 12th, at eleven o'clock they were married in Marylebone Church, with only two witnesses present. Mrs. Browning returned to her home. The exodus of the Barretts was announced for the 21st, but

Browning would not come to the house again—they felt it would not be right for him to do so. On the 19th the lovers fled; they went to Southampton, to Havre, to Paris, and thence to Marseilles by way of Avignon. They coasted from Marseilles along the Riviera to Leghorn, and came to rest in Pisa.

IV

The life in Italy, which was the golden time of Browning's poetry, was somewhat precariously financed. For their expenses, Browning had borrowed £100 from his father, who wished to make it a gift, and they had besides some £300 a year from Mrs. Browning's funds. These funds were not to continue prosperously for more than three years, and though Mrs. Browning got some returns from her books, Browning's income from his was negligible. In 1850, what with the expenses of Mrs. Browning's illnesses and the birth of a baby, they were sorely put to it to make ends meet.[24] A stout heart makes the road easier and Browning had that. It held out through difficulties until in 1856 Kenyon's munificent bequest of £11,000 relieved them of worry.

In April, 1847, the Brownings had moved from Pisa to Florence and by the end of the summer had settled in an apartment in Casa Guidi which was to be their home for fourteen years. From Florence they made summer excursions to Fano, Bagni di Lucca, and Siena, and three times to Paris and London: besides these sojourns they spent two winters in Rome. It was at Bagni di Lucca in 1849 that Browning first saw the *Sonnets from the Portuguese* which Mrs. Browning had written to him in London in 1846. But at the end of their travels Mrs. Browning, at least, always returned gratefully to their large, cool rooms in Florence. They were visited frequently by English friends, such as Mrs. Anna Jameson and Father Prout, and they came to know such English residents in Florence as the T. A. Trollopes, Isa Blagden, Harriet Hosmer, Frederick Tennyson, and Landor. Many Americans also sought them out, and they became close friends with the family of William Wetmore Story, the sculptor. They knew another sculptor in Hiram Powers; and they became friends with G. W. Curtis, the literary man, and Margaret Fuller (Contessa Ossoli), the

---

[24] For the financial difficulties of these years, 1847–56, see *New Letters of Robert Browning*, edited by William Clyde DeVane and Kenneth Leslie Knickerbocker, 1950, *passim*.

socialist of Brook Farm. They were visited in 1858 by Hawthorne.[25] Most of the Americans came to see Mrs. Browning, for Browning in the Fifties was more renowned as a husband than as an author. Of an evening their friends would come in to talk, and to share their chestnuts and wine. By day the Brownings would occasionally visit the picture-galleries or go for rides in the country. The daily routine consisted of reading and writing and lessons upon the piano, given by the poet to his little son, Pen.

In later years Browning was fond of saying that Italy was his university. Italy seemed to give him joy and freedom, and in the long, quiet days in Florence he settled many matters for himself. With the encouragement of his wife his interest in religion revived, as we see in *Christmas-Eve and Easter-Day*, 1850, and in pondering history he concluded that the greatest event of history was the incarnation of Christ with its promise of personal immortality, and the second great epoch was the Renaissance when personality reached its fullest flowering.[26] In these fruitful years he developed his doctrine of human and divine love, and the interrelationship between them. He thought deeply, too, about his own art and about painting. We see him, for example, significantly enough, indoctrinating young Lytton with the poetry of John Donne.[27] All this was of immense consequence as a background for *Men and Women*, the finest flower of his genius.

Soon after their arrival Mrs. Browning became a violent partisan of the Italian Risorgimento. She watched rather feverishly the vicissitudes in the fortunes of the Piedmontese against Austria, and finally put all her hopes in Louis Napoleon. Browning was less of a partisan and more of an observer. Though little appreciated, he must have seemed to Florentines such a poet, God's spy, as he imagines wandering around Valladolid:

> He stood and watched the cobbler at his trade,
> The man who slices lemons into drink,
> The coffee-roaster's brazier, and the boys
> That volunteer to help him turn its winch.
> He glanced o'er books on stalls with half an eye,
> And fly-leaf ballads on the vendor's string
> And broad-edge bold-print posters by the wall.

[25] For a compact account of the Brownings' life in Florence see Ch. 1 of *Letters from Owen Meredith (Robert, First Earl of Lytton) to Robert and Elizabeth Barrett Browning*, ed. A. B. and J. L. Harlan, Jr.

[26] See H. B. Charlton, "Browning as Poet of Religion," in *Bulletin of the John Rylands Library* 27:271–307 (1942–3).

[27] *Letters from Owen Meredith*, pp. 144–5, 187.

If you were in Florence,

> You'd come upon his scrutinizing hat,
> Making a peaked shade blacker than itself.

In his walks he bought rococo furniture for the rooms in Casa Guidi, and once picked up some old paintings that seemed to be the work of Cimabue, Ghirlandaio, and Giottino in a grain-shop a mile outside the city. These rambles were memorable to him. Years later when they were long past he said to his friend, Kingsland, "Oh me! To find myself there, some late sunshiny Sunday afternoon, with my face turned to Florence,—ten minutes to the gate, ten minutes *home!* I think I should fairly end it all on the spot." [28]

This was the even mood of Browning's life in Florence; yet the years were filled with accomplishment and event. In 1849 the first collection of Browning's works had appeared in two volumes over the imprint of Chapman and Hall. It included all his works to that date, save *Pauline, Strafford,* and *Sordello.* The same year was full of joy and grief: on March 9 a son, Robert Wiedemann Barrett Browning, already mentioned above, was born, but soon afterwards the poet's mother died suddenly in England, and he was unable to go home. The blow was hard to bear and his health suffered. Perhaps these portents of mortality joined with the public questions of the day and his wife's piety to produce his next volume of verse, *Christmas-Eve and Easter-Day* in 1850, in which the three aspects of Christianity in the western world, Protestantism, Catholicism, and Rationalism, were put in picturesque fashion before the reader. Browning's preference went to the little Independent chapel, for all its ugliness, for there, it seemed to him, love was most abundant. The poem was a harbinger of the matter which was to make up too much of Browning's late verse. *Christmas-Eve and Easter-Day* had a sale of 200 copies in the first fortnight, and then the sales ceased.

This poem owed little to Italy; but under the warm sky Browning's secular genius now burst into bloom. All of western Europe was laid under tribute for *Men and Women* of 1855. Florence, Venice, Fano, Siena, Bagni di Lucca, and Rome contributed essential poems. Paris was laid under fee: its roar after the quiet of Florence possibly helped in making *Childe Roland to the Dark Tower Came,* that astonishingly modern poem; its pictures in the Louvre may have helped memory to create the haunting masterpiece, *Love Among*

---

[28] W. G. Kingsland, "Robert Browning, Some Personal Reminiscences," in *Baylor University Browning Interests,* Second Series, 1931, p. 37.

the Ruins. London and Florence collaborated in *One Word More.* Married love received such scrutiny as it had not obtained since John Donne died. The British public hardly suspected that it, and not Robert Browning, was on trial when in November, 1855, Chapman and Hall published *Men and Women* in two volumes. Here was the life-blood of a great master: here was truth and beauty, observation, action and reflection, and many varieties of new music. Here were flawless lyrics, and here the poet had perfected his new technique in the dramatic monologue. At last, one may say, Browning deserved the generous praise which Landor (leaving Shakespeare out of the question) had accorded him in 1846:

> Since Chaucer was alive and hale
> No man has walked along our road with step
> So active, so enquiring eye, and tongue
> So varied in discourse.

In *Men and Women* Browning richly endowed English literature, but the British public for ten years took the gift coolly. A few were fervid in their admiration. His old admirer, D. G. Rossetti, was mad with delight; [29] young men here and there began to see his merit, but the applause was far less than full-handed. To an age used to the bardic formality of Wordsworth and Tennyson, Browning's manner was still too new, too familiar and racy, his utterance too broken. It was the manner of the poetry of the future, if they could have but known. Browning knew precisely where he stood and what he was doing, as one may see from the essay which he wrote to serve as a preface to a collection of Shelley's letters in 1851. The letters turned out to be spurious, but the essay stands, and in it the author saw himself as plain as he saw Shelley. One may see the same clear vision in a letter which Browning wrote to Ruskin in defence of his methods in poetry on December 10, 1855, when the great arbiter of taste had objected to certain traits in *Men and Women.*[30] No mere chance led Browning to read *Fra Lippo Lippi,* one of the boldest and freest of his new poems, familiar in manner and racy in diction, to the group gathered in his temporary residence, 13 Dorset Street, London, on September 27, 1855. On this occasion Tennyson read *Maud,* "my little *Hamlet,*" while D. G. Rossetti sketched him. Mrs. Browning and W. M. Rossetti were also present. But though Browning was discour-

[29] See M. B. Cramer, "What Browning's Literary Reputation Owed to the Pre-Raphaelites, 1847–1856," in *Journal of English Literary History* 8:305–21.
[30] See W. G. Collingwood, *Life and Work of John Ruskin,* 1893, pp. 232–5.

aged by the reception of *Men and Women,* it was with no bitterness that he saw his wife's poem, *Aurora Leigh,* go into edition after edition upon its publication in 1856.

Thus it was with mixed feelings towards the British public that the Brownings returned to Florence in 1856. Kenyon's bequest began to make their financial situation easier. They spent some time in Paris and one summer on the sea-coast of France, near Havre. They were enabled to go to Rome for gaiety, and in the summer, when they chose, they took the large and pleasant Villa Alberti, near Siena, as their residence. Here they were near the Storys, and Landor, under Browning's protection now, was a constant vistor at tea. They would sit on the terrace until far into the evening, the fireflies busy in the cypresses, while Landor and Mrs. Browning debated the conduct of Louis Napoleon. She made him "laugh carnivorously" by telling him that he would have to write an ode in honor of the Emperor to humor her. The care which Browning took of the aged Landor shows the younger poet in a most happy light.[31] He always said that he owed more to Landor than to any of his contemporaries, and he took this excellent way of expressing his gratitude. Landor was not easy to care for; he was violent and improvident. Mrs. Browning did not care greatly for him, partly because he was such trouble for her husband, and partly because he was set against the two great passions of her later years, spiritualism and the Emperor of the French.

The years wore on pleasantly and were deeply troubled only by Mrs. Browning's occasional ill health. There were, inevitably, differences in temperament between Browning and Mrs. Browning: he was naturally inclined to seek company and found Florence a little still; she needed the quiet and comfort of home. There were also disagreements of opinion, strongly felt by each, upon such topics as spiritualism, Louis Napoleon, and the bringing up of their son, Pen. But each respected the right of the other to an individual opinion. There were no more "men and women" being written; Browning was discouraged by the reception of his poetry and soothed his restlessness by modelling in clay in Story's studio. In England, however, his fame was slowly but surely growing, and the young men at the universities were beginning to read him.[32] In Florence in June, 1860, he

---

[31] See H. C. Minchin, *Walter Savage Landor, Last Days, Letters and Conversations,* 1934, *passim.*

[32] See M. B. Cramer, "Browning's Literary Reputation at Oxford, 1855–59," in *PMLA* 57:232–40 (1942). When Browning received an account from Chap-

picked up the "Old Yellow Book" from a book-stall, but the subject
was to lie unused for more than four years still. Then suddenly Mrs.
Browning's health began to decline. All private and public sorrows
seemed to combine against her: her father had recently died without having relented towards her; Cavour had died, and things were
going very badly for Italy. In June, 1861, her health took a turn for
the worse; but yet even her ever watchful husband did not suspect
the danger. On the morning of the 29th she died in his arms. The
happy Italian days were over.

V

In August, 1861, the grief-stricken Browning and his son began to
move towards England where the poet had decided to live henceforth. To stay longer in empty Florence was intolerable; to leave it
was bearable and no more. In this mood he quitted the city and never
returned, save in memory. One of his first acts was to have his son's
curls cut and to dress him in boy's clothes.[33] He arranged with Miss
Blagden, the friend of several years' standing who was with Mrs.
Browning in her last illness, that they should exchange letters
monthly, and it is through Browning's letters to this lady that we may
follow his activities and moods during the next ten years.[34] She, no
doubt, in her letters gave him the news of Florence which his hungry
heart desired. Most of August and September, 1861, Browning spent
at St. Enogat on the coast of France with his father and sister for
company, and there on the lonely wind-swept shore the heart found
some degree of healing. In October he came to London, and after a
few months spent in lodgings he settled into the house at 19 Warwick
Crescent which was to be his home for twenty-six years. He was a
neighbor here to Arabel Barrett, his wife's sister, and in her society
he found much comfort.

Idleness was now the last thing to be thought of, though it had
been pleasant enough in Italy. There was much to be done: Mrs.
Browning's *Last Poems* had to be seen through the press, and her

man in 1863, however, there were still unsold copies of *Men and Women* on
hand; see *New Letters*, ed. DeVane and Knickerbocker, p. 392.

[33] See Gertrude Reese, "Robert Browning and his Son," in *PMLA* 61:784–803
(1946), and also Betty Miller, "The Child of Casa Guidi," in the *Cornhill Magazine* 163:415–28 (Winter, 1948–9).

[34] See *Dearest Isa: Robert Browning's Letters to Isabella Blagden*, edited by
Edward C. McAleer, 1951.

writings collected; their son's education, for Pen was now nearing thirteen, had to be taken seriously in hand; and soon a new collection of his own works was called for. This was to be the collected edition of 1863. These things, especially the training of his son, kept him from morbid thoughts, and summer after summer he found pleasure in ranging the coast of France. The more remote his summer quarters the better he was pleased. After his first grief had passed he was persuaded to go into society, and after 1862 he resumed his old friendships and made many new ones. The friends he sought at first were chiefly literary and artistic people.

Browning was only forty-nine when he returned to London to live. The city was not the same place he had left in 1846. The London of the Sixties had assumed much of its modern aspect: it was richer and huger, with perhaps more human débris than ever in its slums. The industrial revolution had done its first work and the pleasant pastures of Camberwell were no more. The gigantic glass-roofed railway stations were the cathedrals of the new age and the coal-smoke went up like incense. Democracy in its fullest modern sense was now politically in its first decade of existence. Disraeli and Gladstone, and indeed all the characters and furniture of the familiar Victorian scene, were now in place and the curtain was about to rise on England's worldly greatness. The air was full of noises and hoarse disputes. Carlyle and Ruskin were the Jeremiahs of the time, but were already a little out-moded. Arnold viewed the gigantic curves of material prosperity too coldly to please the sanguine draughtsmen of those ascending lines. In 1859 Darwin had published his *Origin of Species,* and the rulers of the universe, aghast, peered into the secret of their lowly origin. At the beginning of the Sixties Huxley and Wilberforce were locked in a none too edifying struggle over the theory of evolution. Further, churchmen of all descriptions, High and Broad, and even the Dissenters, shifted uneasily as they saw the rationalism of Germany and France attack with astonishing success the authenticity of the Scriptures.[35]

The shock of this vigorous new world, together with his musings upon life in his summer retreat on the coast of France, produced Browning's next volume of poetry. *Dramatis Personae* is something of a misnomer for the collection of 1864, for the poet is not primarily

[35] For the major direction of Browning's interest in these years see W. O. Raymond's excellent chapter, "Browning and Higher Criticism," in his book *The Infinite Moment and Other Essays in Robert Browning,* 1950. See also C. R. Tracy, "Browning's Heresies," in *Studies in Philology* 33:610–25 (1936).